MICRO MONSTERS

KINGFISHER
LONDON & NEW YORK

Published in the United States by Kingfisher,
175 Fifth Ave., New York, NY 10010
Kingfisher is an imprint of Macmillan Children's Books, London.
All rights reserved.

Distributed in the U.S. and Canada by Macmillan,
175 Fifth Ave., New York, NY 10010

WELDON OWEN INC.
CEO, President Terry Newell
VP, Sales Amy Kaneko

VP, Publisher Roger Shaw
Executive Editor Mariah Bear
Editor Lucie Parker
Project Editor Nam Nguyen

Creative Director Kelly Booth
Senior Designer William Mack
Assistant Designer Michel Gadwa

Production Director Chris Hemesath
Production Manager Michelle Duggan
Color Manager Teri Bell

Library of Congress Cataloging-in-Publication data has been applied for.

ISBN 978-0-7534-6727-5

Kingfisher books are available for special promotions and premiums.
For details contact: Special Markets Department, Macmillan, 175 Fifth Avenue, New York, NY 10010.

For more information, please visit www.kingfisherbooks.com

A Weldon Owen Production
415 Jackson Street
San Francisco, California 94111, USA

Printed in Shenzhen, China, by Asia Pacific Offset.
10 9 8 7 6 5 4 3 2 1
2011 2012 2013 2014 2015

MICRO MONSTERS

KINGFISHER

NEW YORK

CONTENTS

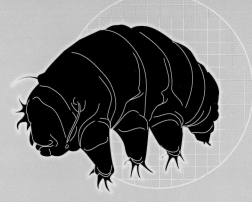

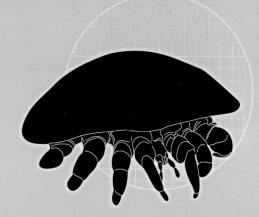

MEET THE BEASTS

Focus your eyes on the world of micro monsters, a realm teeming with creepy creatures that you never knew existed. From tiny insects feasting on plant matter to the nearly invisible beasts that infiltrate our bodies, there are more small critters living on Earth than all other types of animals combined. They may come in small packages, but these fierce warriors use their specially adapted bodies, sharp senses, and disease-carrying abilities to wreak havoc on the larger world around them. What does it take to survive in this strife-ridden realm, where cannibalism is common and enemies are indestructible? Zoom in and discover!

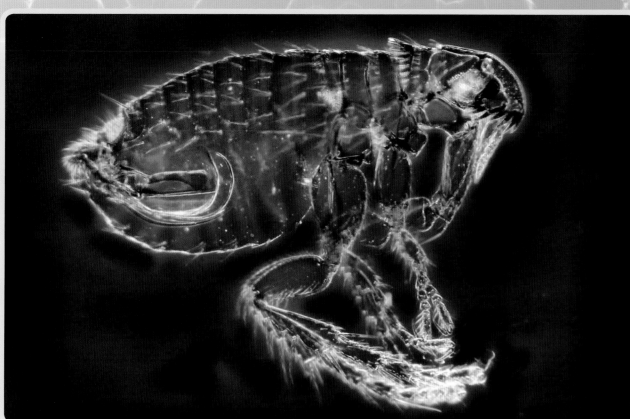

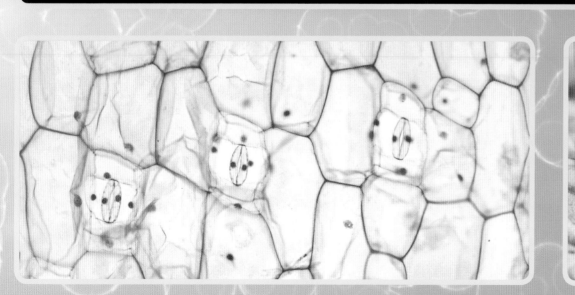

FANGED FLIER

Jumping spiders dominate the spider world—there are more than 5,000 species of these dangerous creatures. Spiders in this family don't sit around on a web waiting for dinner. They stalk their prey, using their powerful legs to propel them forward in a leaping ambush. Then they sink their fangs into prey (some even inject poison), killing their target with one lethal bite.

GEOGRAPHY
Global landmasses except Antarctica

HABITAT
Leaps across semiarid and temperate lands, and tropical forests

JUMPING SPIDER
Salticidae

L: 0.25 INCH (6 MM) **H:** 0.04 INCH (1 MM)

INTELLIGENCE
■■■■■□■■■□■

AGILITY
■■■■■■■■■□■■

STRENGTH
■■■■■□■■■■■■

ENDURANCE
■■■■□■■■■■■■

SPEED
■■■■■■■■■■□

EVASION
■■■■■■■□■■□□

PREY

FLIES
These pouncing predators prey on small insects such as flies, nymphs (insect young), beetles, mosquitoes, and even other spiders.

UP CLOSE

SUPERVISION
Most spiders can only see moving objects, but jumping spiders have great vision. Large front eyes see depth and color, while side eyes gauge distances and have a reflective layer that intensifies light for night vision.

MIGHTY PINCERS
Fingerlike palps hold victims with a fierce, deadly grip.

SNIPER SCOPE
Eight eyes give stereoscopic and binocular vision. Jumping spiders zoom in on prey from 8 inches (20 cm) away.

HYDRAULIC POWER
The fourth pair of back legs provides water-pressurized leaping power.

ANTIGRAVITY DEVICE
Tufts of hair on each leg adhere to smooth surfaces for walking on walls and water.

SUPERPOWER
Incredible leaping ability

EQUIPMENT
Eight legs, eight eyes, fangs, and grasping mouthparts

WEAKNESS
Soft and weak after shedding its skin

FACT
A jumping spider can jump up to 25 times its own length.

BUILT-IN CRANE
A long, hinged neck operates like a crane and a bulldozer to roll up leaves for a nest.

SUPERPOWER
Long reach and power crane

EQUIPMENT
Supersize neck, hidden wings, and thermal-shielded armor

WEAKNESS
Only eats one plant species; will starve if this plant is rare

FACT
Male giraffe-necked weevils wave their necks at each other to establish dominance.

THERMAL ARMOR
Two hard wings create a layer of air that insulates the body from temperature change.

KINETIC PROPULSION
Weevils use their joints like pumps to push air through their bodies.

GEOGRAPHY
Only in Madagascar

HABITAT
Climbs on the giraffe beetle tree in forests and rainforests

HINGED HEAD

This rare and alien-looking creature is found in only one kind of tree in Madagascar, an island near Africa's east coast. The male's amazingly long neck helps him build a home and attract a mate. This swiveling, cranelike neck also makes this long-legged weevil look like a menacing foe, but it eats only plant tissue, seeds, and leaves.

IN ACTION

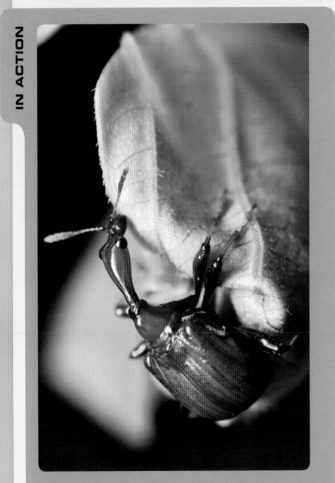

SNUG AS A BUG
Only male giraffe-necked weevils have really long necks. Females choose mates based on neck length and lay their precious eggs in the nests of rolled-up leaves that the males use their necks to create.

GIRAFFE-NECKED WEEVIL
Trachelophorus giraffa

L: 1 INCH (2.5 CM) **H:** 0.25 INCH (6 MM)

INTELLIGENCE	AGILITY
■■■■■■■■■■	■■■■■■■■■■

STRENGTH	ENDURANCE
■■■■■■■■■■	■■■■■■■■■■

SPEED	EVASION
■■■■■■■■■■	■■■■■■■■■■

EXTERNAL SENSORS
Two antennae on the head sense the slightest changes in smell and temperature.

RELENTLESS RAIDER

Swarming colonies of more than half a million army ants can eat an astonishing 100,000 animals a day—which makes them very effective pest control in some places. It may take up to six hours for an ant army to pass through an area, killing all vermin in its way. These eating machines overwhelm prey, often suffocating even large victims with their sheer numbers.

GEOGRAPHY
South and Central America

HABITAT
Marches through tropical rainforests, woodlands, and swamps

ARMY ANT
Eciton burchelli

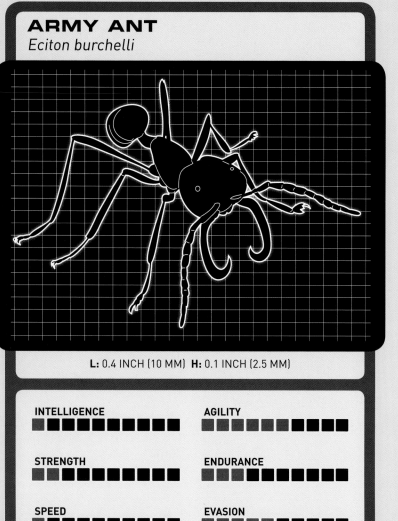

L: 0.4 INCH (10 MM) **H:** 0.1 INCH (2.5 MM)

INTELLIGENCE ▪▪▪▫▫▫▫▫▫▫▫▫

AGILITY ▪▪▪▪▪▪▫▫▫▫▫▫

STRENGTH ▪▪▫▫▫▫▫▫▫▫▫▫

ENDURANCE ▪▪▪▪▫▫▫▫▫▫▫▫

SPEED ▪▪▪▪▪▫▫▫▫▫▫▫

EVASION ▪▪▪▪▪▪▫▫▫▫▫▫

GET A GRIP
Doctors may use the army ant's vicelike jaws to hold a wound closed when stitches aren't an option, letting ants bite the skin together.

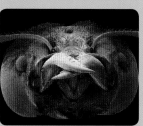

UP CLOSE

IN ACTION

SWARMS AND BIVOUACS
Army ants swarm across forest floors in masses as wide as 50 feet (15 m) across. When ready to sleep, they form tents called bivouacs with their bodies to protect the group, especially the queen.

CHEMICAL TRAIL
Antennae release chemicals that ants use to communicate.

MOTION DETECTOR
Ants' eyes are highly specialized. They can't see shapes, but they can sense all motions.

FUEL DIFFUSION
Ants lack blood vessels. Their hearts pump blood that covers their insides and then drains back to be pumped again.

RIPPING JAWS
Long, curved pincers effortlessly tear apart insect shells.

SUPERPOWER
Overwhelming numbers

EQUIPMENT
Clenching jaws and chemical warfare

WEAKNESS
Extended exposure to direct sunlight is fatal; nearly blind

FACT
Army ants can survive underwater for six hours.

WIND FOILS
Serrated edges and aerodynamic lines in the fly's wings combat wind resistance.

GLOBAL VISION
A fly's multifaceted eyes let it see with almost 360-degree, high-resolution vision.

SUPERPOWER
Bionic eyesight

EQUIPMENT
Giant eyes, task-specific mouthparts, and aerodynamic wings

WEAKNESS
No eyelids; must wipe eyes constantly with feet

FACT
Maggots that hatch in living flesh can be lured from under the skin with a slab of meat.

RUDDERS
Tiny stubs behind the wings adjust to maintain balance during flight.

SOLE FOOD
Sensors on the bottom of a fly's foot let it taste whatever it walks on.

GEOGRAPHY
Global landmasses

HABITAT
Flies around forests, shrublands, and urban areas

NECROMANCER

Flies are associated with death and disease because many fly larvae live off dead flesh or decaying plant matter. Willing to eat almost everything, including dead bodies and human waste, they are considered scavenging vermin around the world. They carry diseases like typhoid, sleeping sickness, and river blindness—along with the waste they eat—everywhere they go.

PREY

APHIDS
Aphids, mites, thrips, and other soft-bodied insects are flies' meal of choice.

UP CLOSE

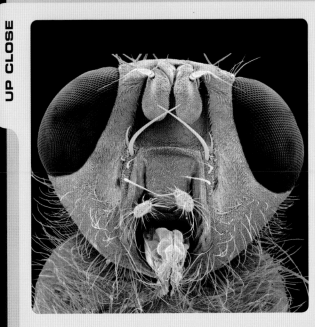

MOUTHPARTS
Flies have special versatile mouthparts that allow them to suck, graze, or drill, depending on what they are consuming. This could be almost anything, including nectar, blood, or flesh.

FLY
Brachycera

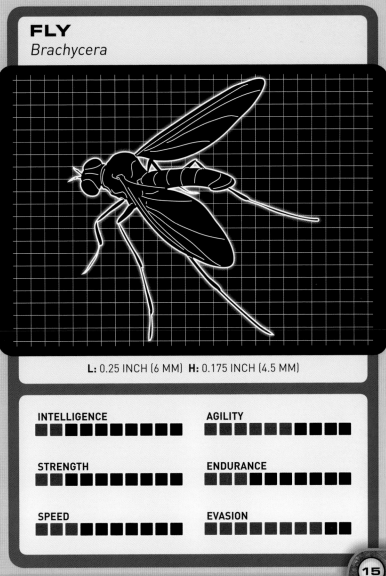

L: 0.25 INCH (6 MM) **H:** 0.175 INCH (4.5 MM)

INTELLIGENCE	AGILITY
■■■■■■□□□□	■■■■■■■■□□

STRENGTH	ENDURANCE
■■■□□□□□□□	■■■□□□□□□□

SPEED	EVASION
■■■■■■□□□□	■■■■■■■■□□

SMALLVILLE

Human eyes are incredibly powerful. They can see details as small as 0.04 inches (1 mm) in size. Here are some tiny creatures that we can see with our eyes—and some creatures that we need the help of science to see.

JUMPING SPIDER
0.25 inches (6 mm), or the width of a thumbtack

FLY
0.25 inches (6 mm), or the width of a pencil eraser

HONEYBEE
0.5 inches (12 mm), or the size of a marble

ARMY ANT
0.4 inches (10 mm), or the width of your finger

TICK
0.2 inches (5 mm), or the length of a grain of rice

DUST MITE
0.015 inches (0.4 mm), or
one-ninth the size of a period

TARDIGRADE
0.02 inches (0.5 mm), or
the width of a pencil lead

MICROSCOPE
...see, scanning
...the rescue.
...ad of light to
...ecimen up
...o allow us to
...isible to us.

BEE MITE
0.06 inches (1.5 mm), or
the width of a knife edge

FOLLICLE MITE
0.015 inches (0.4 mm), or
four times thinner than hair

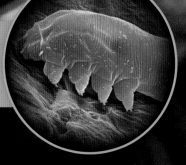

SUPERPOWER
Extreme tracking ability

EQUIPMENT
Two hovering wings, huge eyes, needle-sharp proboscis, and super senses

WEAKNESS
Dependent on water during larval stage

FACT
Female mosquitoes need to drink blood in order to reproduce. Male mosquitoes eat nectar.

NEEDLE ATTACK
A long tube in the mouth contains a pointed knife for piercing. Two serrated cutters on each side slide up and down to slice through layers of skin.

KALEIDOSCOPE EYES
Compound eyes with hundreds of rounded lenses provide excellent vision, even for night hunting.

SUPER SENSORS
Sensitive antennae hone in from a distance of up to 100 feet (30 m) to detect an animal's breath.

GEOGRAPHY
Global landmasses

HABITAT
Swarms over ponds, puddles, and ditches

INFECTION INJECTOR
The mosquito is one of the world's deadliest animals, carrying up to 80 diseases that affect 700 million people each year. They can fly up to 300 miles (480 km) in a lifetime, spreading infection near and far. Though tiny, slow in flight, and requiring very little blood to survive, the effects of the mosquito's bite can be deadly to animals of all sizes.

ENEMY

DRAGONFLY
Dragonflies are one of the mosquito's greatest enemies. They eat up to 50 of them per day, earning them the name "mosquito hawk."

IN ACTION

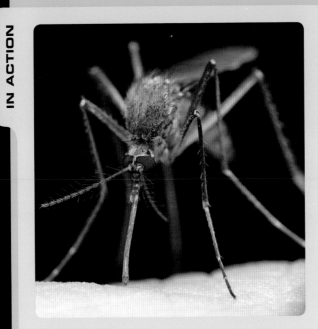

GERM INJECTION
The mosquito's mouth contains two tubes. One drips saliva into a bite wound, while the other sucks up blood like a straw. The saliva tube can deliver germs that cause dengue fever, West Nile virus, and malaria.

MOSQUITO
Culicidae

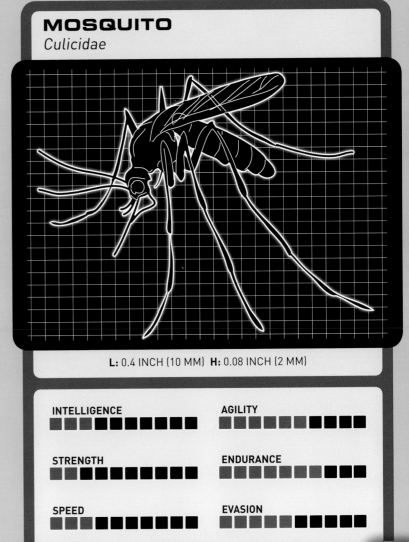

L: 0.4 INCH (10 MM) **H:** 0.08 INCH (2 MM)

INTELLIGENCE	AGILITY
■■■■■■■■■■	■■■■■■■■■■

STRENGTH	ENDURANCE
■■■■■■■■■■	■■■■■■■■■■

SPEED	EVASION
■■■■■■■■■■	■■■■■■■■■■

CHEMICAL WARFARE
Chemicals in a mosquito's saliva keep victims from feeling pain and stop blood from clotting.

SPINAL TAP

Beware the fuzzy caterpillar! That's not fur you see, but dozens of hollow spines that can break off into an attacker or anything that touches it—some species' spines even contain poison. With these defensive spines, caterpillars consume relentlessly and are a scourge to farmers, stripping trees bare in days. Others have become carnivorous, feeding on other insects.

GEOGRAPHY
Global landmasses, especially in the tropics

HABITAT
Inches over trees, leaves, branches, and grass

CATERPILLAR
Lepidoptera

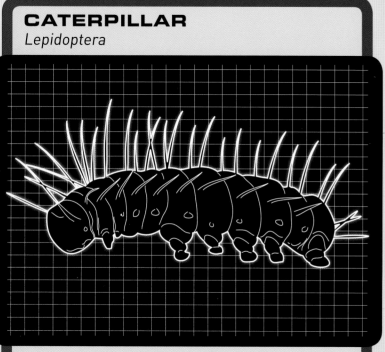

L: 2 INCH (5 CM) **H:** 0.5 INCH (1.25 CM)

INTELLIGENCE ■■■■■■□□□□

AGILITY ■■■■■■■■■■

STRENGTH ■■■■■■■■■□

ENDURANCE ■■■■■■■■■□

SPEED ■■■■■□□□□□

EVASION ■■■■■■■■□□

WASPS
Certain wasps lay their eggs on caterpillars. As the eggs hatch, the larvae feed on the caterpillar until it dies.

ENEMY

UP CLOSE

TOXIC INJECTION
The poison inside some caterpillar species' spines creates a stinging rash if it is touched. Most animals leave caterpillars alone, but skunks eat them after rolling them on the ground until the spines fall off.

BUNGEE CORD
A caterpillar has a special gland in its head that makes silk to protect and anchor it.

POISON HOOKS

Some caterpillars' spikes contain poison. The barbed ending catches and digs into skin.

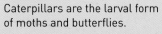

SUPERPOWER
Enormous appetite and growth

EQUIPMENT
Exoskeleton, suction-cup tail, poison spines, and multipurpose silk gland

WEAKNESS
Poor vision; can barely see shapes or shades

FACT
Caterpillars are the larval form of moths and butterflies.

EXTRA MOBILITY

The caterpillar's many limbs have plenty of suction power, allowing them to stick to surfaces and move along.

ADAPTABLE HOUSING

The caterpillar will molt up to five times before becoming a moth or butterfly.

HEATING UNIT
A bee's wings propel it to speeds of more than 2 miles per hour (3 km/h). The wings also produce necessary heat.

UV VISION
The eyes of a bee can see ultraviolet light, and special hairs detect flight speed and wind direction.

SUPERPOWER
Coordinated group attack

EQUIPMENT
Thermal-action wings, auxiliary eyes, and deadly stinger

WEAKNESS
Self-destructs when it uses its stinger

FACT
Bees produce wax and honey from a gland in their legs. Hundreds of bees pool the materials to create beehives.

TRI-EYES
Three ocelli, or primitive eyes, are used to sense light and dark.

KILLER SWARM

Working in groups, bees can devastate enemies. Mass stings kill, but their wildest weapon is heat balling. In this technique, worker bees cook a wasp alive by swarming it and beating their wings to make lethal heat. With 35,000 to 45,000 worker bees in a colony, all equipped with stingers and ready to mobilize en masse, these sweet honey makers are not to be disturbed.

GEOGRAPHY
Global landmasses except Antarctica

HABITAT
Forms hives around trees, roots, and caves

IN ACTION

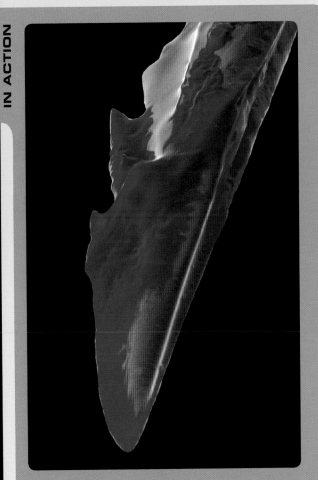

LETHAL WEAPON
Unlike queens and drones, worker bees are equipped with barbed stingers that tear off and work into the victim, distributing venom. This leaves the bee badly wounded, and it dies shortly after stinging.

WIRED FOR SOUND
Auditory organs in antennae hone in on messages from bee teammates.

HONEYBEE
Apis mellifera

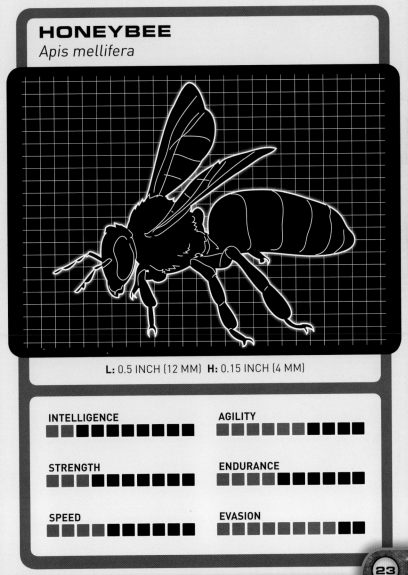

L: 0.5 INCH (12 MM) **H:** 0.15 INCH (4 MM)

INTELLIGENCE
■■■■■■■■□□

AGILITY
■■■■■■■□□□

STRENGTH
■■■□□□□□□□

ENDURANCE
■■■■■□□□□□

SPEED
■■■□□□□□□□

EVASION
■■■■■■■□□□

23

SWEET DESTRUCTION

These destructive mites come from Asia, where bees are resistant to them. But honeybees in North America and Europe have little defense. These mites kill honeybee larvae and disable adults, annihilating a hive within seven months. They infest larval bees and kill or maim them by sucking their blood before they have a chance to emerge from the hive.

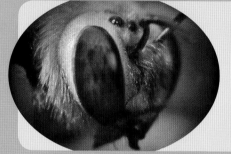

GEOGRAPHY

Asia, North America, South America, Europe, and Africa

HABITAT

Creeps on the bodies of bees

BEE MITE
Varroa destructor

L: 0.06 INCH (1.5 MM) **H:** 0.08 INCH (2 MM)

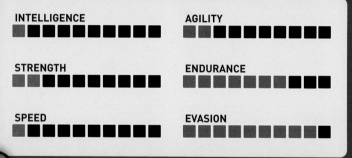

INTELLIGENCE

AGILITY

STRENGTH

ENDURANCE

SPEED

EVASION

DEFECTIVE WINGS
Bee mites are believed to be partially responsible for the recent collapse of bee colonies. The mites damage wings so that bees can't fly.

IN ACTION

UP CLOSE

COLOR CODING
The bee mite starts out white and darkens with age. All red mites are female. Yellow males die when the larval bee emerges, but female mites are able to cling to the bee's body as it grows into adulthood.

SMELLING FEET
The bee mite's nose is in its front two legs. It waves them in the air like antennae to smell.

STEALTH SHAPING
The bee mite's flat body can wedge between a bee's abdominal segments, where the mite is safe from grooming.

SUPERPOWER
Unshakable staying power

EQUIPMENT
Stealthy flat body and specialized mouthparts

WEAKNESS
Dependent on the bee host to develop and mature

FACT
A bee mite can reproduce within ten days of its birth.

LIFE SUCKING
Up to 11 bee mites may feed on a single bee. Mite infestations can reduce a bee's weight by almost 3 percent.

ADHESIVE PADS
A sticky pad on the end of each foot adheres strongly to bee hairs.

SUPERPOWER
Marathon feeding that lasts up to 24 hours

EQUIPMENT
Hard shell, six climbing legs, and bloodsucking mouthparts

WEAKNESS
Inability to jump; can only crawl

FACT
Ticks can carry diseases such as Lyme disease and Rocky Mountain spotted fever.

CLEAT FEET
Hooks and spikes on each foot hold ticks to blades of grass, where they wait for victims.

ARMOR PLATING
A hard tick's back shield is made of strong plates that protect the head and mouth.

SUPERGLUE SALIVA
Two piercing mouthparts secrete saliva that hardens to a cementlike substance, sticking to skin during feeding.

GEOGRAPHY
Global landmasses except Antarctica

HABITAT
Lies waiting in forests, deserts, and savannas

TENACIOUS TERROR

Ticks are so varied, resilient, and adaptable that almost every land creature on this planet is a potential meal source for them. They glue themselves to their hosts when they dive headfirst into meals, and once they latch on, they are difficult to remove. Attempts to pull out these stubborn bloodsuckers may only break off their bodies, leaving their heads behind.

IN ACTION

DIVE IN
A tick feeds headfirst. It takes at least an hour of feeding to transmit diseases to a host. Quick removal will prevent illness from spreading.

UP CLOSE

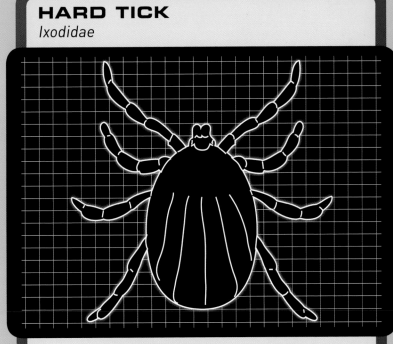

BLOOD BALLOON
Female ticks swell up to incredible sizes after a blood meal. It is crucial that the females consume so much blood, as they need its nutrients to develop the 15,000 eggs that each female will lay.

HARD TICK
Ixodidae

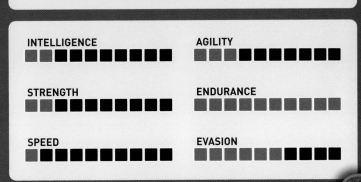

L: 0.1 INCH (2.5 MM) **H:** 0.125 INCH (3.175 MM)

INTELLIGENCE	AGILITY
■■■□■■■■■■	■■■■■■■■■■

STRENGTH	ENDURANCE
■■■■■■■■■■	■■■■■■■■■■

SPEED	EVASION
■■■■■■■■■■	■■■■■□■■■■

STANDBY MODE
When faced with shortage, ticks power down their metabolism. They can live for four years without feeding.

27

SKIN EATER

Numbering anywhere from 100,000 to ten trillion mites per human bed, these voracious creatures don't live on humans—they live next to them, sharing a habitat and devouring the flakes of dead skin that humans shed. With the ability to lay an astonishing 200 eggs per day on beds and carpets, these mites can blanket the entire world.

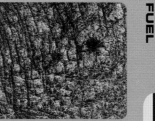

GEOGRAPHY
Global landmasses except Antarctica and dry deserts

HABITAT
Crawls in carpet, bedding, clothes, and furniture

DUST MITE
Dermatophagoides farinae

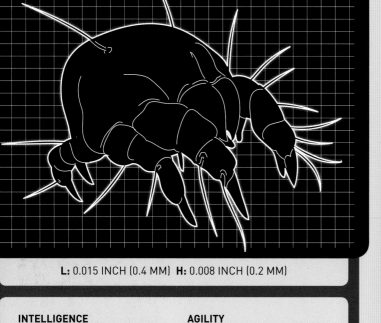

L: 0.015 INCH (0.4 MM) **H:** 0.008 INCH (0.2 MM)

INTELLIGENCE

AGILITY

STRENGTH

ENDURANCE

SPEED

EVASION

FUEL

DEAD SKIN
Dust mites feast off the dead skin flakes that people shed every day. They also drink our sweat by absorbing it through their skin.

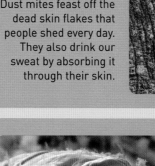

ENEMY

CHEYLETUS
These larger cousins of the dust mite do not feed on human skin. Instead, they practice cannibalism on their dust-eating relatives. They can easily overpower and consume dust mites.

ALL-TERRAIN GRIPPING
Legs with sticky pads on the bottom hold on to any surface, resisting even vacuum cleaners!

BODY ARMOR
A hard yet permeable shell protects the tiny mite from harsh elements.

SUPERPOWER
Massive numbers

EQUIPMENT
Grasping mouthparts, eight sticky legs, and water-sucking armor

WEAKNESS
Requires at least 65 percent relative humidity

FACT
Mites ingest their feces up to three times to extract nutrients and water.

PRECISION TARGET LOCK
Four mouthparts work like fingers and lips to extract and suck up food from microscopic debris.

POWER ABSORPTION
A porous casing takes moisture directly from the air, so mites do not need to drink.

SUPERPOWER
Near indestructibility

EQUIPMENT
Grappling claws, sensitive eyespots, and adjustable skin size

WEAKNESS
Requires film of water over body to prevent it from drying out

FACT
If in danger, the tardigrade can shrivel up and run at 1 percent metabolism.

ELASTIC ARMOR
A nail-like covering can expand or shrivel up tightly to help the tardigrade save energy.

PIERCING ATTACK
Mouth probes are useful for piercing plant and animal cells.

CLONING ABILITY
If a tardigrade is in poor health or cannot find a mate, it will produce clones of itself.

GEOGRAPHY

Worldwide in oceans and on land

HABITAT

Nestles in moss, lichen, soil, ice, and freshwater sediment

IMMORTAL MONSTER

Tardigrades, or water bears, are some of the most resilient creatures known. Able to withstand radiation, vacuum, and extreme cold, they thrive everywhere from the Himalayas to the polar icecaps. Their preferred habitat is moist moss and lichen, but these tough and many-limbed creatures can make a go of it anywhere—even in space.

PREY

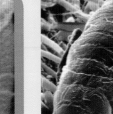

ROTIFERS

These small, industrious animals are not very mobile and make perfect meals for the many-limbed tardigrade.

ENEMY

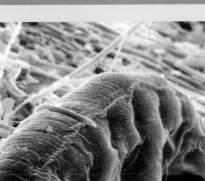

WATER BEARS

If the moss that they live in dries out or freezes, tardigrades begin to starve. To survive these harsh conditions, these vegetarians will become cannibalistic and eat each other.

TARDIGRADE
Tardigrada

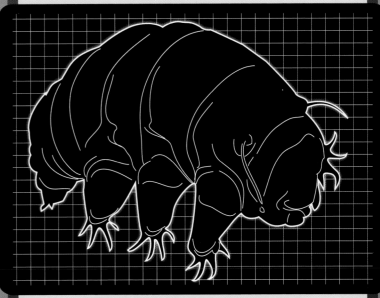

L: 0.02 INCH (0.5 MM) **H:** 0.002 INCH (0.05 MM)

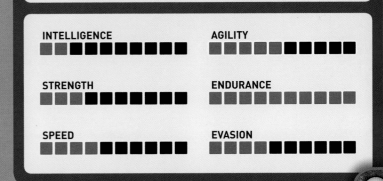

INTELLIGENCE	AGILITY
STRENGTH	ENDURANCE
SPEED	EVASION

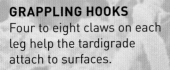

GRAPPLING HOOKS

Four to eight claws on each leg help the tardigrade attach to surfaces.

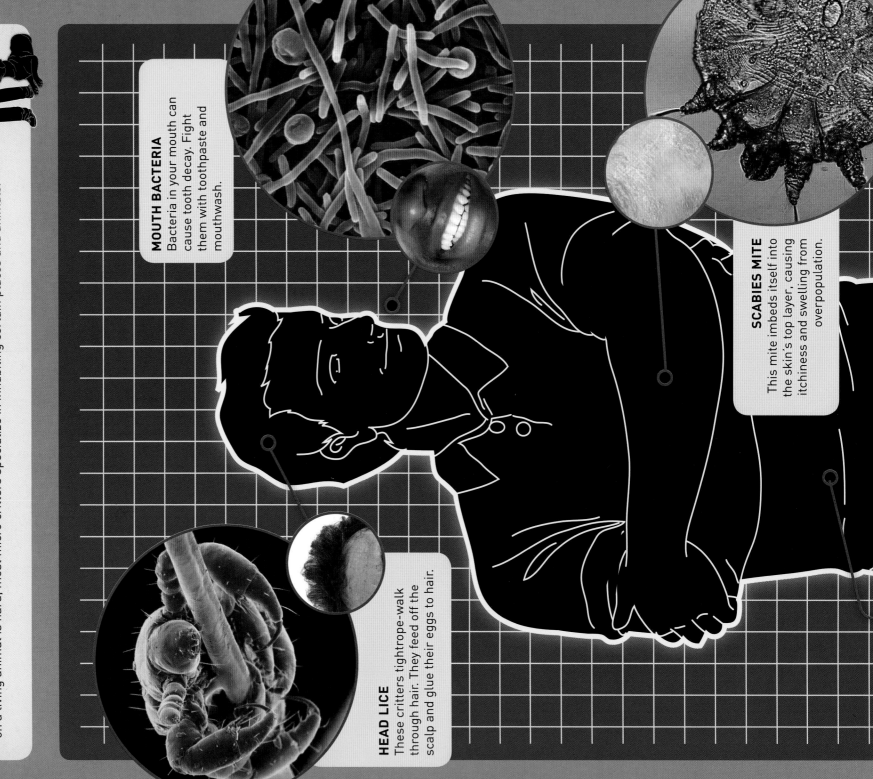

LIFE ON YOU . . . .

Small and microscopic creatures exist everywhere, especially on bodies, which are great shelters and sources of food. There are roughly 200 different species living on or in you. For microfauna, the body is a vast terrain of oceans, mountains, and crevices that constantly changes. Because survival on a living animal is hard, most micro critters specialize in inhabiting certain places and animals.

MOUTH BACTERIA
Bacteria in your mouth can cause tooth decay. Fight them with toothpaste and mouthwash.

SCABIES MITE
This mite imbeds itself into the skin's top layer, causing itchiness and swelling from overpopulation.

HEAD LICE
These critters tightrope-walk through hair. They feed off the scalp and glue their eggs to hair.

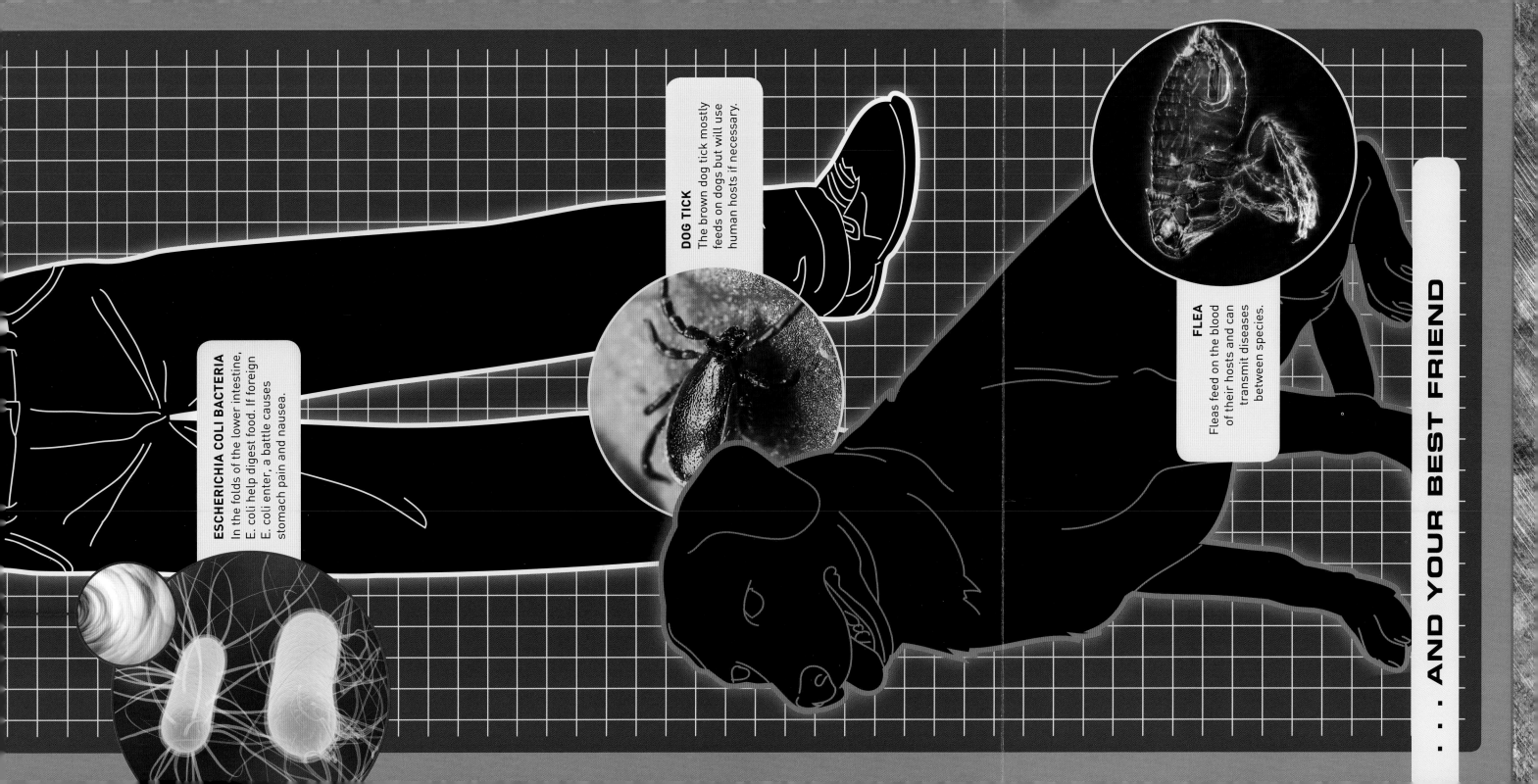

ESCHERICHIA COLI BACTERIA
In the folds of the lower intestine, E. coli help digest food. If foreign E. coli enter, a battle causes stomach pain and nausea.

DOG TICK
The brown dog tick mostly feeds on dogs but will use human hosts if necessary.

FLEA
Fleas feed on the blood of their hosts and can transmit diseases between species.

. . . AND YOUR BEST FRIEND

TRICHOPHYTON
This fungus burrows into skin and causes swelling and an infection called athlete's foot.

NOTORIOUS NIT

Lice infect up to 80 percent of people in some parts of the world. These itchy invaders live on rich and poor people, clean and dirty heads, and short or long hair—but they occur most commonly on children due to the close contact between kids. Head lice are so perfectly adapted to living and ingesting blood on a human host's hair that they cannot survive anywhere else.

GEOGRAPHY
Worldwide on humans

HABITAT
Hides in human head and body hair

HUMAN HEAD LOUSE
Pediculus capitis

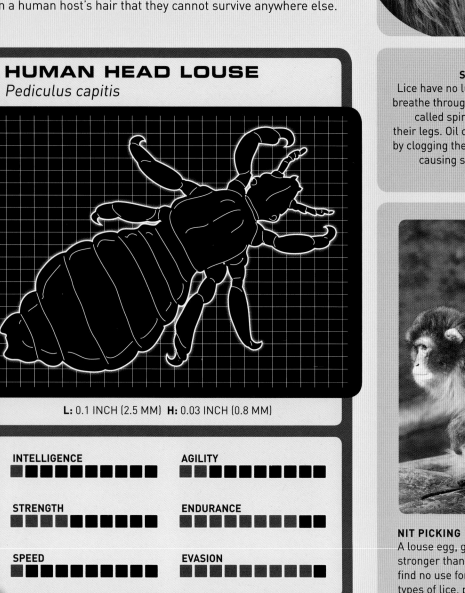

L: 0.1 INCH (2.5 MM) **H:** 0.03 INCH (0.8 MM)

SPIRACLES
Lice have no lungs. They breathe through air holes called spiracles near their legs. Oil can kill lice by clogging the holes and causing suffocation.

UP CLOSE

IN ACTION

INTELLIGENCE		AGILITY	
STRENGTH		ENDURANCE	
SPEED		EVASION	

NIT PICKING
A louse egg, glued to a single hair with a substance stronger than cement, is called a nit. Although humans find no use for lice, other animals, who have different types of lice, pick off the parasites and eat them.

CIRCULAR SAW
Blades inside the mouth roll out to cut and grind skin and then roll back in when they are finished.

EXTRA PERCEPTION
Antennae on the louse's head and legs detect smells and humidity levels.

SPIKY ANCHORS
A louse's mouthpart has sharp points that turn inside out to grip, anchoring the louse's head to its victim's skin.

SUPERPOWER
Creeping infestation

EQUIPMENT
Hooked feet, blunt head, and grinding mouthparts

WEAKNESS
Unable to walk if not on hair

FACT
Lice can transmit typhus, trench fever, and relapsing fever.

ZIP LINE
Each leg ends with a hooked claw that lets lice run forward or backward on a hair without ever having to turn around.

ADHESION STRIPS
Ridges on the abdomen and head help keep the animal from sliding off skin surfaces.

DRILL BIT
The mite's single oral needle extends and retracts to dig into flesh.

SUPERPOWER
Gnashing and liquefying

EQUIPMENT
Long body, oral needle, and cheek claws

WEAKNESS
All waste collects in the body until death

FACT
80 to 100 percent of people over the age of 50 are infested with follicle mites.

PRICKLY SPUR
Follicle mites have small spikes and two-pronged claws to anchor them to skin.

MIGHTY GRINDER
Fat cells and oils are churned and obliterated by seven ridged teeth inside the mite's cheeks.

GEOGRAPHY
Worldwide on humans

HABITAT
Digs around noses, cheeks, foreheads, temples, and chins

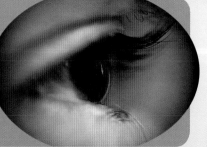

IN ACTION

FACE INVADER

Follicle mites dig into pores headfirst, devouring skin and oil. Once embedded in pores, they can cause acne breakouts and skin inflammation. There is no known way of ridding the skin of them once they have settled. With seven sharp claws and a pointed needle mouth, these mites make short work of feasting and digging through human pores.

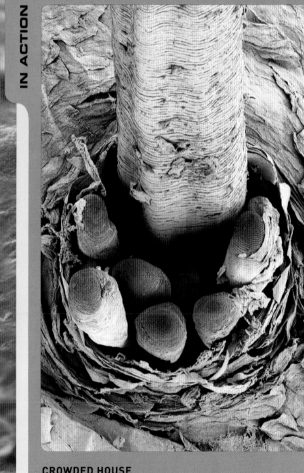

CROWDED HOUSE
Mites in an overcrowded pore will die, and the bodies will contribute to infection, leading to pimples. When mites digest oils, they make a chemical that turns the oils black, which can cause blackheads.

FOLLICLE MITE
Demodex folliculorum

L: 0.015 INCH (0.4 MM) **H:** 0.002 INCH (0.05 MM)

INTELLIGENCE	AGILITY
■■■□□□□□□□	■□■■■■■■■□

STRENGTH	ENDURANCE
■■■■■■■■■■	■■■■■■■■■□

SPEED	EVASION
■□■■■■■■■□	■■■■■■■■■□

ENGULFING ENEMY

Amoebas are an entire group of animals that can shape-shift to eat with extensions of their bodies. They surround food with tendrils, transfer it to the middle of their bodies, and then digest it with chemicals from the outside in. Constantly morphing feelers surround and hold victims, making the amoeba a nightmare for any cell or bacteria.

GEOGRAPHY
Freshwater worldwide

HABITAT
Oozes through ponds, rivers, lakes, and standing water

AMOEBA
Sarcodina

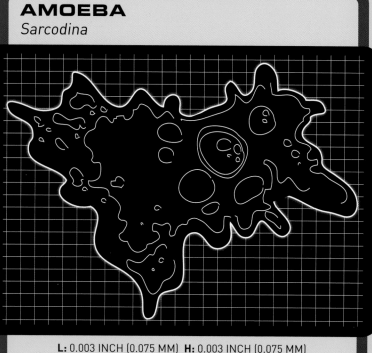

L: 0.003 INCH (0.075 MM) **H:** 0.003 INCH (0.075 MM)

INTELLIGENCE ■■■■■■□□□□□
AGILITY ■■■■■■■■■■■

STRENGTH ■■□□□□□□□□□
ENDURANCE ■■■■■■■□□□□

SPEED ■■■□□□□□□□□
EVASION ■■■■■□□□□□□

ENTAMOEBA HYSTOLYTICA
This amoeba is a human parasite that lives in dirty water. It causes dysentery, killing 100,000 people a year.

HAZARD

IN ACTION

MEALS ON THE GO
An amoeba engulfs its prey and deposits it in a bubble called a vacuole, where it is stored as the amoeba moves around. When hungry, the amoeba floods the bubble with digestive chemicals that dissolve it.

FALSE FEET
Pseudopods extend and retract from the body like feet in order to move. They also engulf food like a mouth.

ENVIRONMENTAL ENERGY
An amoeba's membrane absorbs sugar and water directly from its outside environment.

SMART BOMBS
Amoebas use lysosomes to dissolve prey. This protein makes cells explode, clearing tunnels into flesh.

SUPERPOWER
Movement in multiple directions at the same time

EQUIPMENT
Pseudopods and liquefying lysosomes

WEAKNESS
Can only live in fluids

FACT
Bacteria are an amoeba's main food source. They also feast on algae and plant cells.

NUCLEAR FISSION
To reproduce, an amoeba doubles the size of its nucleus and then splits into two animals.

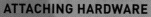

NEXT GENERATION
Each tapeworm segment can change sex from male to female and fertilize the eggs in a segment next to it.

ATTACHING HARDWARE
Hooks and suckers on top of the head stick to intestine walls, ensuring that the worm is hard to remove without breaking.

SUPERPOWER
Amazing self-generation

EQUIPMENT
A single head with a hooked surface and many flat egg-carrying segments

WEAKNESS
Extreme vulnerability to toxins

FACT
A tapeworm can have up to 4,000 segments, and each segment contains thousands of eggs.

MODULAR SURVIVAL
Although they function as a whole, if separated, each segment can form an entire new tapeworm, complete with eggs.

AMBIENT POWER
Tapeworms have no stomach because they can absorb and digest all nutrients from their surroundings.

GEOGRAPHY
Worldwide in oceans and on land

HABITAT
Hitches onto the intestines of humans, cattle, swine, and fish

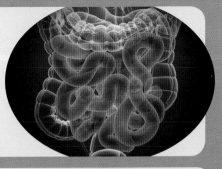

HOOKED HORROR

Tiny tapeworm segments affix themselves to intestine walls with hooks and feed off of nutrients inside the body. There they grow into long, winding forms that release up to 300,000 eggs a day. Easily passed from animal to animal by undercooked meat or direct oral contact, these sticky parasites are survivors of the most invasive and repulsive kind.

UP CLOSE

MEASURING TAPE
Tapeworms circle inside the intestine, and hosts rarely know they are infected unless a segment breaks off in stool. While tapeworms enter the body as incredibly tiny segments, they can grow up to 32 feet (10 m) long.

TAPEWORM
Cestoda

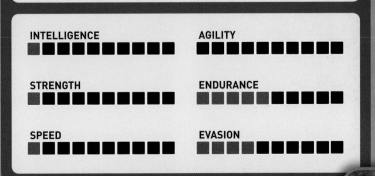

L: 0.02 INCH (0.5 MM) **H:** 0.002 INCH (0.05 MM)

INTELLIGENCE	AGILITY
STRENGTH	ENDURANCE
SPEED	EVASION

VEINOUS ASSAULT

Schistosomes, or blood flukes, affect over 100 million people worldwide, entering through infected water or food. They cause abdominal pain, intestinal bleeding, and anemia. If they get lost, they may enter the brain, where they will form cysts. Although blind and toothless, these bloodsuckers wield spines and a suction cup to tear through veins, wreaking havoc on hosts.

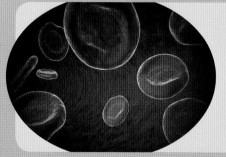

GEOGRAPHY
Africa, South America, Middle East, and Asia

HABITAT
Siphons the blood vessels of humans, rodents, and cattle

SCHISTOSOME
Schistosoma

L: 0.5 INCH (1.25 CM) **H:** 0.009 INCH (0.23 MM)

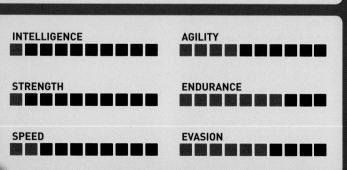

INTELLIGENCE
■■■□□□□□□□□

AGILITY
■■■■■■□□□□□

STRENGTH
■■■■□□□□□□□

ENDURANCE
■■■■■■■□□□□

SPEED
■■■□□□□□□□□

EVASION
■■■■■■■□□□□

PREY

FINAL HOST
Final hosts pick up the worm through infected snails or water. The worms mate inside the host and release eggs into the urine or feces.

IN ACTION

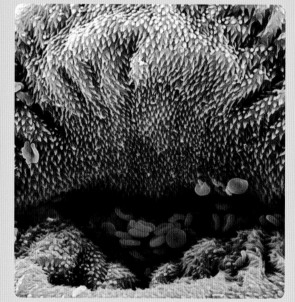

OXYGEN BAR
Schistosomes do not have blood. Instead, they eat the blood of their hosts and use it, as if it were their own, to circulate oxygen throughout their bodies.

REGENERATING SKIN
The skin sheds every few hours to get rid of host antibodies that attack the schistosome.

SUCTION CUP
A schistosome's large sucker on its stomach docks it to blood vessel walls while eating.

BRISTLE MOUTH
Spines cover the head and mouth and work like brushes to sweep blood cells into the gut.

SUPERPOWER
Transfusion, uses blood of host as its own

EQUIPMENT
Attaching suckers and toothy spine brushes

WEAKNESS
Needs water snails to grow

FACT
Schistosomes are specialized to prefer livers, bladders, or intestines, but all feed on blood.

LIFE MATES
Male schistosomes have a structure that wraps around the smaller female. They stay connected and reproduce for their entire lives.

DRONES

BUBONIC PLAGUE
Host: Fleas, rodents, and humans
Name: *Yersinia pestis*
This bacteria creates swollen glands and lesions. If unchecked, it will spread and cause death. It killed one-fifth of Europe's population in the mid-1300s.

TOOTH CAVITIES
Host: Any organism with teeth
Name: *Mutans streptococci*
This type of bacteria, the only kind able to grow on smooth tooth enamel, makes a film for other bacteria to grow on. Bacteria digest tooth enamel and leave holes in the teeth called cavities.

PLANT NODULES
Host: Legumes, beans, and potatoes
Name: *Rhizobium* and *spirulina*
Bacteria converts nitrogen from the air into solid fuel that some plants need to survive. Plant roots called nodules house these bacteria.

WHAT ARE BACTERIA?
These single-celled organisms live everywhere, and most are beneficial. But some types invade animal or human bodies and start reproducing in enormous numbers that overwhelm the systems of their hosts. Others even make powerful toxins that damage body tissue and cause illness. Luckily, bacteria can be treated with antibiotics.

WHAT IS A VIRUS?

The hacker of the micro world, a virus is a DNA fragment that hijacks cell centers in its host, using them to reproduce en masse. Since viruses are just pieces of code (not living creatures), antibiotics cannot be used to kill them—only the immune system can defeat them.

FOOT-AND-MOUTH DISEASE

Host: Cows, sheep, pigs, and other cloven-hoofed animals
Name: *Picornaviridae Aphtovirus*
This virus attacks hoofed animals, targeting cells in the skin, nose, hooves, mouth, and ears. The virus bursts cells, creating open sores that spread the disease to other animals.

COMMON COLD

Host: Primate noses
Name: *Rhinovirus*
Rhinoviruses are highly contagious. They attack cells in the nose, sinuses, and throat and cause them to swell. This swelling causes symptoms like a runny nose, sore throat, and sneezing.

CHICKENPOX

Host: Humans
Name: *Varicella-zoster* virus
This airborne virus lives in the respiratory tract. Infected nerves cause rashes called shingles, while infected skin shows itchy spots called chickenpox.

GLOSSARY

abdomen The third segment of an insect's body, following the head and the thorax.

aerodynamic Designed to decrease wind resistance. A fly's wings are aerodynamic.

antennae A pair of special body parts that contain organs for sensing smell, sound, touch, temperature, or taste. Most animals with antennae have them on the top of their head. Ants use them to receive the chemical signals that their colony-mates use to communicate.

antibody Any protein made by a creature in defense against an antagonistic and invasive agent.

auditory This term refers to something that is related to, or experienced through, hearing.

bacteria A whole group of microorganisms that come in rod, spiral, and round shapes and live in colonies in air, water, ground, or animal bodies.

bacteriophage A type of virus that targets and infects bacteria. Found almost everywhere, these organisms are one of the most versatile and diverse specimens on the planet.

binocular A type of vision in which both eyes are used simultaneously to create a single image. This trait allows for a greater field of vision.

bivouac A temporary shelter that army ants build by linking their bodies together, creating a protected space where army members can rest and that protects the queen ant.

cannibalism An animal eating another animal of its same kind. Dust mites and a few other species of micro creatures have been observed exhibiting this behavior.

carnivore An animal that eats mostly meat, though its diet may include other types of food such as plant matter.

colony A group of animals of the same species that live, find food, and defend themselves together, such as ants and bees.

compound eye An eye made up of many separate lenses. The lenses see in different directions, creating super-high-resolution vision. Most insects have compound eyes, but mammals have eyes made out of single lenses.

dengue fever A disease carried by mosquitoes that causes fever, joint pain, rashes, and vomiting. In more serious forms it can cause internal bleeding and death.

diet The type of food and drink regularly eaten by an animal.

exoskeleton A hard, defensive exterior shell that protects animals such as caterpillars.

eyespot A tiny organ that cannot see but can sense light in order to move toward or away from it. Eyespots are most common in more primitive animals such as the tardigrade.

fangs The long, sharp, needlelike teeth that some animals use to grasp, tear, or bite their prey. Jumping spiders use them to inject venom.

habitat The place where an animal is best suited to live. Common microscopic animal habitats include hair, skin, intestines, and blood.

hair follicle A tube of hair cells surrounding an inner shaft. Many types of mites live on hair follicles throughout the body.

heat balling In this process, certain types of bees group together and surround an enemy wasp. Then, with buzzing wings, they create enough heat to cook the trapped wasp to death. This is the bee colony's only chance to defend itself from a wasp, and it is an important weapon—a single wasp can defeat an entire colony of bees that do not have this defense in their arsenal.

herbivore An animal that eats only plants.

host A living animal or plant on which a parasite lives. The final (or definitive) host is the animal in which the parasite develops to maturity.

insect A member of a group of animals with no backbone, six legs, and three-part bodies. Army ants, giraffe weevils, and bees are types of insects.

keratin A type of protein that comes in the form of fibers. Different arrangements of the fibers make up soft hairs on a bee and pliable cuticle skin on a tardigrade.

larva The immature, wingless, often wormlike form of an insect that hatches from an egg. This larva changes form and molts before transforming into a pupa or chrysalis and, finally, into an adult.

light microscope An instrument using light and lenses to make small objects appear larger.

Lyme disease A disease carried by ticks. It causes a rash, followed by fever, aches, headache, and swollen joints. Joint pain and heart problems may show up throughout an infected person's life unless the disease is treated.

lysosome A small packet containing material that liquefies proteins. Amoebas use lysosomes to digest their prey.

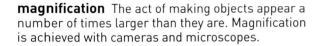

magnification The act of making objects appear a number of times larger than they are. Magnification is achieved with cameras and microscopes.

malaria A type of disease caused by blood parasites that are transmitted through a mosquito's bite. Malaria causes fever and aches and can be lethal if it is not treated.

microscopic Something that cannot be seen by the human eye without the use of a microscope.

molting The periodic shedding of a creature's outer layer—many micro monsters molt numerous times throughout their lives.

mouthpart A protrusion from the mouth that assists a creature in spearing prey or moving.

nit These eggs of a louse are whitish, almost clear sacs glued to the hair shaft.

nucleus The central control center of a cell that directs the cell's growth, energy expenditure, and reproduction. An amoeba's nucleus splits in two, forming two separate amoebas.

ocelli Small, simple eyes found in animals without bones and many insects. An ocellus consists of one single lens and a few sensory cells.

palp A short, leglike structure near a spider's fangs that helps it sense the nearness of prey and judge when to bite.

parasite Any creature that lives on, in, or with another animal or a human and depends on it for food, protection, or something else it needs to survive. Sometimes this relationship is mutually beneficial, but other times parasites harm or do not affect their hosts.

permeable Having pores that allow liquids or gases to pass through. The skin of a tapeworm is permeable so that food can pass directly through it into the worm's gut. The shell of a dust mite allows water to pass directly through it so the mite does not have to drink.

predator An animal that hunts and kills other animals for food.

prey Animals that are targeted, hunted, and eaten by other animals.

proboscis A long, tubular part extending from the mouth. Mosquitoes have piercing proboscises that allow them to sting their prey.

pseudopod A temporary, footlike protrusion that allows amoebas to move and to envelope prey.

Rocky Mountain spotted fever A disease caused by bacteria carried by ticks. A major carrier of the disease is the Rocky Mountain tick. A rash develops where the tick bites. If untreated, the rash will turn black as skin starts to die.

saliva A mixture of fluids that is secreted from the mouth. Saliva contains chemicals to dissolve food but can also contain other special ingredients. The saliva of ticks hardens to cement, and the saliva of mosquitoes keeps blood from clotting.

scanning electron microscope A type of microscope that uses a focused beam of electrons to reflect off an object in order to create an image on a screen. Scanning electron microscopes (SEMs) can resolve details many times smaller than a light microscope can.

seta A rigid or bristly body part. Some animals, like the dust mite, have setae that act as sensors.

silk A fine, continuous fiber made from protein. Insects such as spiders and caterpillars produce silk to make webs, cocoons, and safety lines.

spiracle Holes made for breathing that are often found in insects along the legs, thorax, or abdomen.

stereoscopic An attribute meaning that something—whether a pair of eyes or a microscope—is capable of seeing, recording, or in another way processing three-dimensional images.

stylus A hard, pen-shaped mouthpart. Many microscopic predators have styli for piercing and puncturing.

typhus A disease caused by bacteria carried by lice. The symptoms are high fever, rash, difficulty swallowing, and mental confusion.

ultraviolet A wavelength beyond the range of light that humans can see. Bees have eyes that can see ultraviolet as a visible color. Many flowers have ultraviolet patterns that draw bees to them.

venom A poisonous substance that bees and some other animals inject into their prey in an effort to disable and dominate it.

virus A type of microscopic complex that can only reproduce by using structures of living cells. Viruses cause many illnesses, including the common cold.

West Nile virus A type of virus spread by mosquitoes to humans and birds. The virus causes fever, aches, rashes, and swelling of the brain.

worker bee A type of female bee. Unlike the queen and drone bees (whose sole responsibility is reproduction), worker bees gather pollen for honey.

CREDITS

All illustrations by Liberum Donum (Juan Calle, Santiago Calle, Andres Penagos).

All images courtesy of Shutterstock Images unless noted below.

Getty Images: 24 middle

iStock Photos: 38 middle and bottom; 44 top; 48 main

Nature Picture Library (Richard du Toit): 45 top

Photolibrary: 6 top; 18 main; 30 main; 35 main; 36 main; 43 main; 44 bottom

Science Photolibrary: front cover; back cover top right; 6 bottom right; 7 top right; 9 main; 12 middle; 15 bottom; 16 center; 17 main, top right, bottom right, and bottom left; 21 main; 22 main; 23 bottom; 24 bottom; 25 main; 26 main; 27 bottom; 31 middle and bottom; 32 all large images, except for E. coli and flea; 36 main; 37 bottom; 39 main; 40 main; 41 bottom; 42 bottom; 45 center; 47 top middle and top left

ACKNOWLEDGMENTS

Thanks to Jacqueline Aaron, Justin Goers, Emelie Griffin, Bret Hansen, Stacy Luke, Sheila Masson, Susan McCombs, Elina Rubuliak, and Brandi Valenza.